ALL MEN ARE LIKE FLIES

"I think Eddy Duhan is a better writer than Tom Waits!"
Nik Venet (Legendary producer, Capitol Records, The
Beach Boys, Bobby Darin, etc...)

"I have had 3 other songs written about me Eddy, but
yours is the best one of them all!" Harriet Schock (Multi-
platinum, award winning songwriter.

"Yeah Eddy, this is very personal... for sure there's some
really touching stuff in the book... I read the first 5-6, then
skipped thru and read 7-8 more including the last
four. "All Men Are Like Flies" could resonate with a lotta
people and become an underground hit." Wayne Zeitner
(Marketing and Development of Veggie Tales, Fancy
Monkey, and Thomas Nelson.)

"Eddy sings like he talks... he recites poetry with a guitar
in his own unique way, and does it with a certain passion.
It's kind of like John Fahey meets Charles Bukowski."
John Andrew Schreiner (Keyboard player and record
producer.)

EDDY DUHAN

All Men Are
Like Flies
and other long lost
poemsongs

ISBN: 978-0-9829059-0-6
Long Lake Publishing
longlakemusic@yahoo.com

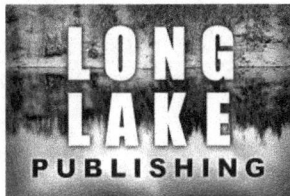

*Acknowledgements and Inspiration; William Blake for
"Songs of Innocence and Experience". Charles Bukowski
for; "Burning In Water Drowning In Flame", and
"Besieged".   John Fahey for; "How Bluegrass Music
Destroyed My Life", and "Vampire Vultures", The House
of Daniel family, John Andrew Schreiner, and the Great
Bible Poet Himself.*

This book is dedicated to
Sarah and Jan

Introduction

I was born in Sudbury, Ontario. My father worked at the Inco mine. He died when I was 3 years old, and we were uprooted back to North Battleford, Saskatchewan, where my parents came from. I was the youngest of 5 children. I am of Ukrainian ancestry, and my family is from a long line of farmers from the Ukraine and Saskatchewan. I left home at 15 with my childhood friend Sherman Doucette. We hitchhiked to Vancouver together in 1969. Sherman had a cheap guitar, and I played it until my fingers bled! The first songs I learned were "Positively 4th Street" and "Get Back". When we got to Vancouver, Sherman and I parted company. Sherman followed the hippie road and went to Kool-Aid. (He eventually became a professional blues harmonica player). I went to the House of Daniel and became a Christian. Let's see, I went back to school, took some college, I attended the same church as Peter Fox and John Fluevog, and worked for them in Gastown and Victoria after the House of Daniel disbanded.

I was very influenced by the lively worship choruses that I heard back then. The first Christian song I learned was "We Are One In The Spirit". I also wrote my first song but for the life of me I cannot remember it! I do have this faint memory of being in an attic in Toronto when I was 16, then finding a big box of stolen dictaphones up in that attic, and singing the song into one of them. Then I remember something about the guy who stole them getting caught and going to jail...So that was my first poem/song and my first recording. It's funny how some things get started!

(This friend at the House of Daniel in Vancouver was praying one time and came up to me afterwards with this wild look on his face and told me that God spoke to him, saying we were supposed to go to Toronto together to start the House of Daniel-East! So we hitchhiked across Canada together in the wintertime. We picked up 3 others in Edmonton who wanted to come along too, and as you probably know 5 people can't hitchhike together, so I ended up going it alone. I think that is where I really learned to trust in God).

We failed miserably at starting House of Daniel-East. It ended up with 12 of us were living together in an attic on Heron Street, and eating peanut butter and porridge every day. So after a fight broke out and someone got thrown down a flight of stairs, I went back to Vancouver. I hitchhiked back again the next winter. Yes, I hitchhiked across Canada *twice* by myself in the wintertime...On the way to Vancouver, I stopped in at Saskatchewan to see my mother and stepfather to tell them that I had become a Christian and wanted us to get along, and love one another like Jesus wanted us to. My stepfather grabbed me by my shirt and threw me out of his house into the snow, yelling at me; "I'LL GIVE YOU JESUS IF YOU WANT LOVE! GET OUT!'" So I slept shivering in a house down the street that was just being built with bare plywood walls and no insulation. In the morning I moved onward to Edmonton where I ran into my brother and sister. They pooled their money together and bought me a new guitar. It was stolen from the House of Daniel the day I arrived back there. They were in the process of closing down and wharfing into Daniel's Place; a coffeehouse in Gastown with craft shops. I began playing songs and reciting poetry there with a friend who kept the rhythm by beating on an MJB coffee can. Ah, such comedy! (A number of years ago I attended a House of Daniel reunion in Stanley Park, and this lady named Rose walked up to me and said, "Eddy, God never meant for you to start the House of Daniel East. He gave that job to me. He just wanted you to plant the seed." And what a hard seed it was, but what a beautiful rose that grew.) I also learned how to do leatherwork from Ken Rice.

After that, I moved to Edmonton and opened Elisha Leather and Coffeehouse, and started a Christian newspaper called, "The Reality" with Peoples Church. I also got involved with the Agape Force in Edmonton and attended their DTS in Tyler, Texas. I played regularly at their "Underground Railroad" with a group called "Gospel Pie". I also played at "The Hovel", and "Room at the Top"(University of Alberta). I traveled around a lot during those days sharing Jesus and doing concerts in coffeehouses, and churches around Vancouver, Toronto, Winnipeg, Victoria, Edmonton, and Kelowna. In Kelowna I was part of a trio called, "Spirit River" with Warren and Jude Hansen (Candle, Agape Force) and they introduced me to David Burgin (Joy, Blessed Hope).

Eventually, I moved to California at the prompting of my college professor, and the influence of friend Dave Burgin. Dave introduced me to Terry Sheppard (IAM Studios), and Gary Arthur (The Way), and Gary introduced me to Jeff Lams (Benny Hester, Donna Summer). I was living on the YWAM ship in Long Beach harbor at the time working with the electricians trying to get it sea worthy. Jeff Lams needed a room-mate so I moved in with him after the MV Anastasis set sail, and through Jeff I met record producer John Andrew Schreiner. I also started working with Thom Roy at White Field Studios, which was owned by the Swedish singer, Evie Tornquist. Thom introduced me to Jan Wilson from KDOC-TV, and he asked me to show her how to operate our Chyron. We started dating after that. I took a job with GTE (Verizon), and have been there for about 24 years now. I also attended the Recording Engineering program at Golden West College.

I started a group called, "The Homeless Drifters" with Robert McGee, and we played everywhere, like the Troubadour, McCabe's, Gypsy Den, the Basement, the Centerfield, you name it (Once we even played at a lesbian bar in LA and they kicked us off the stage for singing about Jesus-lol!). Unfortunately, the Homeless Drifters was short lived...

Then as a member of NARAS, I was privileged to participate with legendary producer, Nik Venet (Capitol Records, The Beach Boys, Bobby Darin, etc...), and Harriet Schock ("Ain't No Way To Treat A Lady") in "The Campfire Conspiracy" (which became "Grammy in the Schools"), and it was a very great learning experience for me!

During that time Jan and I were married, and we had a beautiful little girl named Sarah Elizabeth.

I also continued to work with good friend John Andrew Schreiner on songwriting and publishing projects. John and I wrote "Creation Song" together and it went to #1 for Fernando Ortega. One of the greatest things for me is when we get letters from churches and choirs asking if they can use our songs in their worship to God. Recently, John and I adapted the "Odes of Solomon: The First Christian Hymnbook" to music (TheOdesProject.net).

This book is a compilation of poemsongs that I've written over the years starting with probably one of the first poems I wrote when I was 15 at the House of Daniel called, "All Men Are Like Flies". Not too long ago I received an email from an old friend from the House of Daniel days who wrote; *"Hi Eddy, I was going through a box of old things, and found a poem that you wrote when we were living at the House of Daniel. I don't know if you still have it or not or remember it, but here it is: Did you ever make it into a song?"*

So thank you Charlotte, for the inspiration to do this book of long lost poemsongs! Eddy

contents

1.

2.

3.

4.

1.

When you see the extremes of what humans can be,
both at the same time from degradation to glory...
and the tension in between
that pushes you either way.

all men are like flies

all men are like flies
caught in the web
of the world's lies
woven by their
foolish pride.
each night
and every morn
souls to misery
are born
each morn
and every night
souls are born
in sweet delight!
but whether born
day or night
to misery
or sweet delight…
all men are like flies
caught in the web
of the world's lies,
woven by their
foolish pride.

The House of Daniel, 1969.

widows walk

standing up on widows walk
on one summers morn.
I came upon the same odd thought
I had one time before…
the wind was blowing hard that day
it really blew my mind,
to watch the pearls being cast away
and trampled by the swine!

we're all living in the time of Daniel,
when kingdoms rise and kingdoms fall.
we were living in the House of Daniel,
to read the writing on the wall.

_The House of Daniel, 1970

besieged by Bukowski

this wall is green
that wall is blue
these walls have ears
they have eyes too.

this wall frames my mother's face
this wall a sheet of frozen ice
the other wall is melting wax
my father's bones spill from the cracks.

outside is the city
more cruel than any walls
almost nothing is far better
than nothing at all.

never dare to venture out
disconnect the phone and lower the shades
it creeps to the call of bells and lights
the city is an open grave.

and the last wall will crawl
with angry famished spiders
finally the walls are all we have
to remain within and hide forever.

ode to Blaise Pascal

I stumbled upon Blaise Pascal
in a church near the Pantheon.
between the two eternities
of minuteness and the vast unknown.

standing on the edge of time;
at the point where they both meet.
between matter and the mind
we walked in from a sunlit street.

the church bells began to toll
at 17 minutes after 2.
a strange time to be chiming,
as if to say hello to you…

diversions paths are like a magnet,
to pull you off of your course.
like disdainful armies marching,
through wildflowers of true north.

the telescope that sees eternal
the microscope eternal too.
the milky way, the one cell atom,
all point to God, and God to you.

stained glass windows

stained glass windows
looking outward
shining in the afternoon sun.

like gemstones
in a glass of wine
reflecting the end of time.

one day I will stand
at the end of the rainbow
with you…

misfortune

I had a reoccurring dream
I wake up long ago
music playing in my head
like a transistor radio
across from a wheat field
swaying in the wind
on a hot summer afternoon
and I am only ten

break on through to the other side
sing voices from the ground
imagination running wild
there's no one else around
a battle for the soul
with a pick-axe and a shovel
breaking up the ground
between Jesus and the Devil

misfortune
the funny bone of tragedy
misfortune
I once was blind but now I see
misfortune
life springs from the misery
misfortune
can break a chain and set you free

Mother Nature says to me
it's time to go to school

when you're burning like a flame
it's hard to keep your cool
misfortune wants to kill me
it's tried a time or two
I've got the scars to prove it
but still the sky is blue

I'm pulling up the roots
with matches and some water
it's funny what can make you laugh
when things are getting hotter
so I walked out to the highway
and got a ride back up the hill
in an old green and blue sedan
with a kind stranger at the wheel

Lilith

sometimes you lose your mind
and then it all works out
so you try going back to find
what it was all about
you remember all the pain
spread out across the floor
you remember all the passion
but can't feel it anymore

there's a picture of Lilith
hanging on the wall
a head with five eyes
yet she didn't see the fall
you pick up the telephone
but you struggle with the call
because ever since Adam
nothing's changed at all

when you only see the fragments
there's an urge to connect the dots
with the loss of faith complete
you want to fill in all the spots
it's like finding the old photos
long after someone died
these lost wisps of magic
to light the flame inside

there are brushes in the corner
yellow feathers silver spoons
two fingers and a thumb
head with partial hose
cage free caffeine
Curious Nick and chocolate shoes
artist as early man
gummies cake and worms

so I dialed the number
"hello mesh" she said
but I didn't answer
I just hung it up instead
it's been just too many years
to conjure up the past
where there is no future
and the present has been cast

eye contact

restaurant car jock
frantically wipes off
small screen TV.
with a Kleenex.
"YEAH, 75 TO 63!"
he shouts at me
in a voice similar
to Don Knotts.
couple walking
locked together
moving fast
across the boardwalk.
woman clicking
man shuffling
out a rhythm
on the sidewalk…

but I'm thinking about you tonight,
tension resolve focus and light.
so many things want to pull you from sight,
but I'm thinking about you tonight.

eye contact
I remember
eyelids fall
like fading embers.
red sky spread
across horizon

leaves turning
into autumn.
eye contact
I remember
days and nights
locked together.
cloud formations
cover skies
shadows falling
over eyes…

and I remember
eyes wide open
blazing sun
burning bright
and I remember
love exploding,
tension resolve
focus and light.
and I remember
truth unfolding,
eyelids open
blind to sight.
like waves crashing
on shore at night,
into dancing water
morning light.

down in Jamaica

de hotel and da lawyer
and de revenue man
shake it with da dealer
all hold out de hand
shake out de downtrodden
he's got no place to stan.
Jamaica es movin'
like a cruise ship on lan.

down in Jamaica
dey do what dey can
to keep de cash cruisin'
and shake dat money stick, mon!

shake on de tourist
skakin' da bean
shake out de ganja
shake dat tree kleen
shake off de algae
indigenous man
Jah, don't let dis cruise ship
go down again!

ode to Henry Miller

he was an artist
who lived in Big Sur
painted for passion
wrote for his life
memories of Paris
Tropic of Cancer
Hieronymus Bosch
the man with four wives.

like Picasso and Steinbeck
all rolled into one
pulling his cart in a jock strap
up a mountain in the afternoon sun
the fruits of paradise
the millennium
trying to restore his soul back to nature
where the lion lays down with the lamb.

but there was a devil in paradise
who fell like lightening in the first earth age
to be bound in chains for a thousand years
and shortly thereafter cast into the flames.

he was an angel
born in the flesh body
the paint of creation
source of his light
memories of heaven.
the struggle for beauty

big empty beaches of Big Sur
waves crashing on life.

alarm clock birds

5 am
and the sparrows were singing
outside the window.

there was this old Greek lady

with a thick Greek accent
that lived down the stairs
underneath
me and my old roommate,
Jeff Lams.

"SHUDDUP YA STOOPID BIRDS!"
she yelled out her window.
then she would stamp her foot
trying to scare the sparrows away.

Jeff played the keyboards
so he would practice
on an electric piano
with the sound turned off
at 9 pm
at night
in the darkness
in his bedroom
(this was back when he was playing
with Benny Hester
and just before he started playing

with Donna Summer.)

she would take her
broom handle and start banging on her ceiling
underneath him.
Jeff came out of his room and said to me, "Can you
believe this?"

one day Benny
came over

at 2 pm
on Saturday afternoon,
and asked me if I wanted
to hear the new test pressing
of "Legacy".

"sure" I said.
so we put it on at low volume
and sat on the couch.

within 5 minutes
the old Greek lady
came running up the stairs
"coulda ya turn da music down.
it too LOUD!"

so Benny turned it off halfway through a song and
said,
"maybe some other time, I'm gonna fly."

"sure." I said.

then he left.

the next morning she was out there yelling again.

"SHUDDUP STOOPID BIRDS! SHUDDUP!!"

shortly after that, Jeff and I flew too.

mother nature

every time Mother Nature
has PMS!
it's like John the Baptist,
and the said Herodias;

it stretches back to the garden
and sex with the Devil
now guarding at the entrance
the flaming sword of an angel.

so sing a song if you can,
until the storm clouds overthrow.
the earth turns with a Passion
and the sweat of the brow;

the children have come to the birth
with no strength left to deliver.
like a raft in the darkness
on the rapids of the river.

when Mother Nature rages
then Mother Nature teaches,
but how did she get this recipe
to bring forth such poison peaches?

mythology

it's that old mythology
of spring and summer fall and winter
the cycles of life baby
romance comedy tragedy satire

we made it through the seasons
the changes in the weather
it's like the old saying goes
what don't kill you makes you stronger

it's the battle of the sexes
of war and peace love and hate
the storm clouds pass eternal
but hope springs from the gate

it's that old mythology
of light and dark black and white
like the trickster and the phoenix
and love rains down in archetype

under the mission bells

under the mission bells
of San Juan Capistrano
ringing with the morning prayers
of a sister of constant sorrow
a little bird just flew away
it was time to do the same
as a dark shadow falls
across an oncoming train

there was nothing in the paper
there was nothing to explain
just a girl from Chula Vista
and nobody knew her name
a stranger on the track
behind the yellow tape
a lost soul jumped off the platform
trying to escape

I wonder if she'll be missed
I wonder who's to blame
for such a bitter pill
of self-hatred and disdain
like a fallen angel
racing toward the light
and step into eternity
with every demon that you fight

I hope somebody loved her
as they watched her grow

I hope she'll be forgiven
for what she didn't know
imbalances in nature
reaping what you sow
it's never a simple matter
when someone just lets go

this old house

this old house is still standing,
on the hillside of the prairie.
in the whitewood and red berry,
like a fragrance of a memory.
from prairie wool to wheat dust,
it carried you away-
and if these grey boards could talk,
I wonder what they'd say?

life is a circle,
and we all come back here someday

now buried in the tall grass,
these combines and tractors,
cement truck and ambulance.
stoves and refrigerators.
junk cars and lawnmowers,
blacksmith shop with useless tools,
barking dogs and rusted gears.
to hunters and collectors-

life is an auction,
we bargain to buy back the years.

so I've come back to this land,
to search for memories of my father.
the beam that held up the house,
servant of God and master carpenter.
yet the things I seek to know,

are the things I've always known.
until the crooked be made straight
until we reach our eternal home-

life is a doorway,
you can never pass this way again.

prairie town

I've seen the sun go down
on a wind-swept prairie town
I've seen what it can do to the mind
some tossed in a quarter
some tossed in a nickel
and some tossed in their dreams every time

the stores have all closed on main street
the only one left standing is the pawn
there are generations buried in the graveyard
and all the coins in the wishing well are gone

the Wal-Mart is a fortress
it's the last stop on the highway
a place where you can find the hangers on
the farmers are all worried
they've never seen much Farm-Aid
except maybe in a country and western song

I grew up in this town
when life was all around
we played in the streets 'til after dark
and I wish that I could go there
back to the way it was before
when I ran with my old friends around the park

theme from black and white tv...

Perry never lost a case,
James always got the girl.
Friday always solved the crime,
Dr. Evil never ruled the world.

black and white tv,
made it hard to see.
the shadows on the wall,
how life would really be.

underneath the surface,
underneath the rug.
down past hole in the basement,
where the silver spade once dug.

it¹s a little shop of horrors.
with monsters in hard light,
but for candy colored clowns,
it¹s a wonderful life...

stolen pencil

you kind of remind me,
of Jean Val jean.
you stole my pencil,
and it stabbed me,
in the heart.
blood dripped on the pages,
of the diary.
and wrote these words-

maybe she'll call me,
maybe she won't.
maybe I'll go,
for a walk out on the pier.
drink some coffee,
watch the surfers float,
Venus and Mars,
are looking mighty clear.

call my brother,
way up there in the north.
he's all covered up,
in a blanket of snow.
like coyotes howling
across the prairie tonight
we talk about people
that we used to know...
"Hey, do you remember Jean Val jean?"

write her a letter,

write her a song,
write her a poem,
about love gone wrong.
draw some flowers,
sketch a solitary rose,
or just send back this pencil,
that I presupposed.

she never called him father

she never called him father
she never called him dad
but she cried at his funeral
some things are just too sad.

he used to beat his daughter
once he hurt her pretty bad
he put her in the hospital
and claimed that he was mad.

once he even raped her
tore away her innocence
some souls are lost forever
without redemption or forgiveness.

now she wants to bury the past
forget what happened at his hands
so he can never touch her future
at least that much she understands.

they said his own father beat him
and his mother was as hard as nails
now he's in the hands of God
and the Devil's in the details.

the big lie

you can find it on the internet,
like a crazy quilt in chain stitches
Billy Graham a freemason!
the Clinton's illuminati witches!
Bush Dynasty drug lords,
911 done by Jews
and Jesuit Society of Jesus
shadow government makes the rules.

the big lie the big resolution
control every situation
create the problem and solution
destroy every institution.

third temple scam distraction,
sons of Cain the handlers
of cabbages and kings,
congressmen and governors.
neo-cons and vile liberals
Black Pope behind the Vatican
Jerusalem the world capitol
like tools in the Devils hand.

here comes the one world government!
the beast and the Club of Rome
new world order with no borders,
United Nations Skull and Bones.
Protocols of the Elders,
Satanic ritual Bohemian Grove

HAARP tampers with the weather
digital angel tracks every move.

whatever happened to Marilyn Monroe?

call the press corp
call Jeraldo
got this burning question
everybody wants to know…
calling Oprah
or the doctor who was in charge
calling Elvis
just don't call Wally George!

and tell us
what ever happened to Marilyn Monroe?
her spirit still haunts us
she wants us to know;
the Kennedy's, the Mafia, and the CIA.
there's a skeleton in the closet
is it LBJ?

what really happened with JFK
was it Romeo and Juliet
or did they just get in the way
of Dimona, the Mossad and the NSA

were they all in bed together
why won't anybody say_
what really happened to Marilyn Monroe?

heroin

heroin
she screams at you,
from a deserted road…

heroin
don't believe the lies,
that she has told…

heroin
you could love her,
but you'd lose your soul…

heroin
she'll cry I love you baby,
then take control…

heroin
feels like sex.
feels so wet…

heroin
you could ride her,
like a bullet train of regret…

animal dance

lovers on the knife edge
hunger for romance
hunters to the drum beat,
it's the animal dance!
the moon is relentless
at tracking down the heart
and love is the weapon
that tears it apart.

when love goes all the way
it's hard to make it stay
the losers want another chance
and are caught in the rhythm,
of the animal dance!

cars pour onto the boulevard,
from the heat of the parking lot.
escaping flames that felt so warm,
grew to burn raging hot.
rage against the lonely heart,
rage against the dying heat,
raging rhythm of the night,
when two more lonely dancers meet...

a tragedy

pull the nose hairs from your nose
your Pans are falling off!
got plumbers down to Uranus
do something about that cough.

you look as bad as Hades
when are you going to shave;
and replace the Muses that you sent
to an early grave.

hear the Nymphs Echo
when love goes down the well,
swing the bucket down the hole
like a tolling bell.

they say that we were happy
like sardines in a can;
Poseidon and Amphitrite
in Delphinus constellation.

running naked on the sand
by the big old sea,
like petty gods in a pagan play
Aphrodite's tragedy,
that's me!

down in the one way streets

to see the way some people live
through a telephone technician
wading through the garbage maze
to fix a phone in the kitchen.
the bell was not ringing
so he pulls it from the wall
to find a million roaches
between the hammer and the bell.

down in the one way streets
there isn't any doubt;
that there's only one way in,
and there's only one way out.

they shot him in the back
while he was working up the pole
they thought he was a cop
putting bugs on the phones.
so he hung there like a sign
saying: "THERE"S NO 2 JOBS THE SAME!"
but this was just another drive by
this time the cops were to blame
for when they posed as repair men
and used their good name,
down in the one way streets…

the East

the East is red,
the red wants beef.
the beef is a burning wind,
with no relief.
but I've seen Jonah,
underneath the gourd,
saying,"long live America,
until the early worm gets the bird!"

well the sun beat down,
and the wind blew like crazy!
withered all the grass,
burned down the house on the prairie.
it came up fast,
went down faster!
I always thought that God was joking,
about much cattle on the pasture!

they float in the junk,
fill up their pockets.
sail out the cows,
heat up the rockets.
while Deng Xiaoping rides,
the red horse like a cowboy.
singing, "Love me tender,
baby O baby!"

the art of deceit

trust me baby!
don't worry about that call.
go back to sleep;
it was nothing at all!
just turn the other way,
and believe what I say,
trust me baby,
trust me...yea!

forget about that nightmare,
there was no one really here.
you never saw anything!
have I lied to you before?
I was never in the Red Army,
I don't know what you mean.
no one's breaking down the door,
it was just a dream!

while you were looking north,
the viper was at your feet.
you should have been more careful!
with the art of deceit.

waist deep in the big money

I was living down
on the losing end
I didn't have a nickel
didn't have a friend
everyone else
was getting so fat
I was just another
little boomtown rat

they were waist deep in the big money
holding out their hand saying
"what you gonna gimme?"
waist deep in the big money
don't matter how you get it
when you're shaking on the tree

don't sing those songs
that Pete Seeger wrote
if there's a politician here
he'd like to buy your vote
because they don't care
where you dump the waste
time is money
and money makes haste

so they drive around
in the big Cadillac
got a trunk full of money
stashed in the back

well mr. king of the hill
you can kiss my stash
keep your hands to yourself
don't touch my sack

waist deep in the big money
holding out their hand saying,
"gimme, gimme, gimme!"

Jackson, Tennessee

I met this banjo picker
wannabe stand-up comic
in Jackson, Tennessee,
and he invited me over to jam
at the mortuary
where he worked
in the evenings...

I showed up at midnight
he showed me around
he showed me the caskets
the caddies and the cheap ones.
("if you got to go you might as well
go in style", he joked.)

so we sat in the receiving room
and played gospel music
to the soon departed.

then a cockroach
ran across the floor
stopped
and gave us a dirty look
so we chased him
into the bathroom
to the sounds of
Deliverance...
cornered him
and killed him.

then gave it
a fit burial with
a quick flush
to a fine gospel rendition
of "Glory Hallelujah!"

fortunately,
there were no other dead bodies
in the mortuary that night.

after that
we sat on the slab
drank Coca-Cola
and I laughed at a lot of his dumb

mortuary jokes

"a fat middle aged woman had a heart attack and
was taken to the hospital.

while on the operating table, she had a near death
experience. Seeing God, she asked, "Is my time
up?"

God said, "No, you have another 23 years, 2
months and 8 days to live."

upon recovery, the woman decided to stay in the
hospital and have a face-lift, brow lift, lip
enhancement, boob job, liposuction, and a tummy

tuck. After her last operation, she was released from the hospital.

while crossing the street on her way home, she was hit and killed by a car.

arriving in front of God, she demanded, "I thought you said I had another 20 odd years! Why didn't you pull me out of the path of the car?"

God replied, "I just didn't recognize you!"

"and did you hear the one where a Christian man had just died and was on his way to heaven. When he got to the gates of heaven he met an angel. The angel asked him what God's name was.

'Oh that's easy,' the man replied, 'His name is Andy.'

'what makes you think his name is Andy?' the angel asked incredulously.

'well, you see at Church we used to sing this song 'Andy walks with me, Andy talks with me!"

"How did disco die?"
"In the disco inferno."

drum roll and cymbal crash!

good-bye!

the thief and the dog

I was in Houston, Texas
on sort of a missionary trip
with the Agape Force.
it was my first time in Houston

we pulled our van
into a supermarket
parking lot
to get some food
to do some laundry.

this car pulled up
slowly beside us-
and two old ladies were walking by.

then exploding in a succession
like fast moving frames...

a man jumped out of the car
ran up to the old ladies
and grabbed one of their purses!

she fought to hold on to it but lost
so we jumped out of our van
and chased the thief
back to his car.

nervously, he turned and pulled a gun
so we backed off with hands in air...

early the next morning in the projects
we had a prayer meeting
and we prayed for the man
who was probably a junkie.
and we prayed for the old woman
who was on welfare.

then outside the house
on the street
a car hit a dog.
the dog began making these
enormous noises.
so we stopped praying
an all went outside
and dragged the dog off the street.

someone went inside
to call the SPCA
but they didn't want to come
so we called the police
but they wouldn't come either.

so one of the guys
who was an ex-biker from the Hells Angels
decided to put the dog out of his misery.
he found a big 2 by 4
and hit the dog
as hard as he could
across the head
but the dog didn't die

so he kept on hitting him and hitting him
and the dog howled louder, even hideous.
then quietly resigned himself
to the pain
as the rest of us watched;
horrified,
overwhelmed,
paralyzed…

so the ex-biker took the dog
and threw him into a big plastic garbage bag
and left him there
for the garbage man to deal with
eye closed, still breathing, blowing red,
approaching death.

just then these 2 helicopters
circled like vultures
above the sagging streets
as their searchlights
danced
between the buildings
and the ground.

beautiful face

lost on beautiful face
pink in number eight-
20 to win but she only placed
at Hollywood Park today.
she was not a winner
but that's the way it goes,
worth the price of a lesson
to lose by a nose.

68 Cadillac

I think I'll make some money,
and find a place to live.
instead of having nothing,
I'd have something I could give.
I wanna be like other folks,
not different anymore.
I'm tired of runnin' from the cops,
and sleeping in my car.

I'm livin' in a '68 Cadillac,
stare into the rear view mirror.
but there ain't no turning back,
when your livin' in a '68 Cadillac.

preacher on the radio,
says he's worried about my soul.
tells me that I shouldn't
listen to rock and roll.
well I been to hell and back
and I'd sure like him to know
rock and roll ain't nothing
when you're worried about your soul.

so Sunday I'll go to church,
Monday I sing the blues.
Tuesday I'm at the beach,
Wednesday I read the news.
Thursday I met a little lady,
Friday we danced all night!

Saturday she was gone,
but you know that's alright.
cause I'm livin' in a 68 Cadillac...

she blew an engine on the freeway,
I had to leave her sitting there.
walked to the nearest exit,
Lord I didn't have a prayer.
I'd like to thank my guardian angel,
for taking me by the hand,
and pulling me out of the fire,
and out of the oil pan...

you know, one time I even ran into Elvis, he was
hitching down the Golden State freeway...he said,
"Eddy if ya take me to Vegas, I'll buy you a brand
new Cadillac along the way!" so we stopped in at
that dealership in Barstow, with that big flashing
sign right next to the golf and country club. the
salesman says, *"hey Elvis, if ya buy this here
Caddylac from me, I'll even throw in a couple of
these here tees that you can put yer bells on*! Elvis
just smiled, shook his head and said, "Eeee,
what'll they think of next?!"

my lonely room

I'm sitting by the window
in my lonely room
it's the place I need to go
to write a song to write a poem
it's not a place I love to be
or a place I call my home
it's a place to contemplate the heart
and the winds that strip us to the bone

in my lonely room
I see the sun and the moon
the world is still and fixed in place
a bolt of lightning in empty space

I heard all the news today
while listening to the radio
I didn't like what it had to say
so tell me something I don't know
Jeffers wrote in lonely blood
Hank wrote in a skid row room
Moses wrote about the flood
underneath the desert moon

so I'll think about your eyes
as pools of love and innocence
and all the colors of your soul
like flowers by a picket fence
I don't know why it is
but I'll be back here soon

I'll keep your picture on the wall
in my lonely room

for Michalina

you remind me
of a house in Amsterdam
lace curtains
black cat in the window.
the scent of flowers
rising from the yard
a choir chair
swinging on the patio

and when I looked into your eyes
soft moony beams in the lacquer
sitting watching all of those passers-by
like the ghost of Ann Frank's sister

you brought a tear
to my eye
what you said
made me cry
you made me remember
my grandmother
and the smile that she left
when she died

and when I looked into her eyes
soft moony beams in the lacquer
sitting watching all of us passing by
like the ghost of Ann Frank's sister

Nik Venet's dog

I got a call on my voice mail,
just the other day.
this guy said, "this girl said,
for me to tell you to stay away!"
but the last time that I talked to her,
was over three months ago.
except for the other night,
when I called to let her know.
about this black dog in her neighborhood,
but she wouldn't even take the call.
he said, "her family friends and authorities,
already knew about it all!"

romantic christian anarchist,
everybody knows that you're dangerous,
we got your name on the list,
romantic christian anarchist!

the first time that I met her,
she kicked me in the back.
so I wrote her a love letter,
to throw her off the track.
of this hound of heaven,
who was chasing at her heels.
when she said, "everything comes so easy!
and I don't know how it feels."
well if you don't know how it feels,
and you really want to know.
walk through these flames of passion,

that makes all greatness grow.

so we did each other a favor,
if you know what I mean.
like the chisel and the hammer,
and the piece that broke away clean.
and sometimes I don't even think of her,
when I hear that black dog howl!
so I stand like a statue in the corner,
but can't picture her at all.
like so much art misunderstood,
or Picasso just plain odd.
a lot of poop happens for the greater good,
when every blow comes from the hand of dog.

first day on the new job

I met her at the
Holiday Inn
Halloween.

we had set up
our first paint stray gun sale
in the convention room
Sweetroll Roy and I...
Sweetroll was teaching me the ropes

it was my first day on the new

sales job-

her friend was a waitress
in the restaurant.

the telephone rang
3:00 am
my partner Sweetroll
woke me and said, "It's that
girl you met today, she wants

to talk to you…"

 "I want to know
if you'd like to
come over and see
my costume? It's
real sexy!" she said.

I mumbled something ineligible
into the phone
about pagan sex holidays
and woke the next
morning still clutching
the receiver.
and wondered if I had
been dreaming...

we left that town
with 27 thousand cash
in a briefcase.
"Man were you outta your mind-
what was that crap you were talkin'?
she was hot for you!

why

didn't you go over to her place?

I would have covered for you!"

"Well, I'm a Christian," I told him,
"and I don't go

for that kind of swinging,

Sweetroll!"

poetry reading

last night I dreamed
of a house long forgotten,
Peggy was sitting
alone in a chair.
she said, "I can see
that you finally hit bottom,
but I'm glad to see
that you made it back here.
so we climbed up,
through the secret passage,
to those pleasant
but dusty hidden rooms.
and we stood out
on our own private balcony,
and kissed each other
under the smiling moon.

on a cold dark street
somewhere in Edmonton,
you disappeared
into thin air without me.
so I found myself lying in a basement
dead as a skeleton,
tying to learn how to play the guitar
like John Fahey.
I could almost hear
the dry bones rattle,
from a mighty wind blowing

in the valley of vision.
I staggered
under the weight of glory,
like Blind Joe Death
in a transfiguration.

so I made it downtown
to a poetry reading,
some guy was yelling,
"Don't you know who you are?"
He started jumping around
like a wild animal dancing,
so I sold all my records
and gave away my guitar.
it made all my Italian neighbors
nervous but happy,
and I wrote you a letter
to tell myself why.
It took twenty years later
just to finally reach me,
in this dream with these feelings
to which I could never reply.

It was like the perfect landing
in zero visibility
couldn't even see the runway
when the wheels hit the ground.
you said, "Oh, what a pilot,
always one step ahead of insanity,
didn't think that you'd make it

or ever live to touch down!"
but this house
was never built on security,
as we wandered
through the fleeting rooms
and we stood out
on our own private balcony
kissed each other
under the smiling moon.

women are evil-men are stupid

I was somewhere between sleeping
and being awake-
then all of a sudden I was being choked!
by a scaly demon, a devil from hell.
trying to force down these two poison pills.
it said, "women are evil-men are stupid!"

I managed these words with all my might;
"THE BLOOD OF JESUS!
THE BLOOD OF CHRIST!"
a cold death blow to any imp-
it broke its hold at this point.

I puked out the pills in a cesspool flood
as I watched the vile monster
slither away defeated.

then, everything became calm and clean
and I still don't know if it was just a dream...
since it happened with eyes wide open
in broad daylight.

a tank full of blues

two teenage sisters
from a hard rock town
up in the blue northern
guaranteed to grind you down
raising Cain in a graveyard
at 13 after 12
drinking hard whiskey
from the wishing well

a tank full of blues
and a stolen car
one to work the pedals
the other one to steer
they ran out of gas
by the side of the road
there's a body in the trunk
and Sherman Tank Doucette
is on the radio

who broke the banjo
that was hid under the bed
the evidence is not talking
at least that's what they said
they found them by the train yard
hiding in the weeds
waiting for the redeye
where the darkness bleeds

they said he tried to rape them

with a rusty nail
so the cops let them go
instead of sending them to jail
now one works at the diner
where salesmen come and go
and one is on the highway
running from a ghost

Victoria's Secret

we went to the mall
to buy a gift
for a new baby girl
at the Disney store.

little pink dress
little pink socks
chocolate cigar
a flower box.

I sat on the bench
by Victoria's Secret
laid the bag down
and waited for my friend
this guy around twenty
came out of Victoria's Secret,
and pointed at my purchase
and said, "Is that my bag!?"

"What? No-it's my bag." I told him.
then he reached down, and grabbed it!
he tried to look inside
but I held on tight
then I hit his hand
and said, "LEAVE IT ALONE!
what's the matter with you?
are you some kind of moron!?"
then as quick as he came,
he turned and was gone

hey, look out Faye Wray
here comes King Kong!

2.

For innocence
every day seems like an eternity

for experience
eternity seems like a day

for innocence
everything is larger than life

for experience
life is larger than everything

into this world

happy little baby,
dancing in the light.
through pink and yellow flowers,
Godzilla nowhere in sight.
no one ever knows,
just what lies up the road.
the mountains and the valleys,
on the way back home.

into this world we come,
piping loud with glee,
reaching for those everlasting arms,
ah, don't let go of me...

murder in the cathedral!
devoured by your own.
ghosts in the tower!
dignity on the run.
you know but do not know,
see but do not see.
the air is heavy and thick,
with the restless movement of feet.

is this where life begins?
like a picture in a soft gold frame.
and time slips by like a crystal wind,
between what you lose and what you gain...

my little girl

I worry about my little girl
growing up in these times
beyond the trips to Disneyland
ladybugs and nursery rhymes

things it seems are getting worse
than when I was a child
with terrorists and pedophiles
and college girls gone wild

so what should I tell my little girl
I know it's best to tell the truth
but let her be a kid for as long
as she can hold on to her youth

I will tell her that I love her
and help her keep in mind
that as horrible as this world can be
there's beauty at the same time

I will teach her to pray
for God's help in every quest
give her flowers on the special days
and just keep hoping for the best

find a name

it's hard to find a name,
for a baby on the way.
you think of possibilities,
of what the name should say.

a name from the Bible,
a name of renown.
worthy of the poets,
how does this one sound?

but what is in a name,
other than what you invest?
to make it so great,
the child that is blessed.

so God bless this child,
with the faith of an Abraham.
God bless this child,
with Solomon's song,

God bless this child,
in the name of Jesus,
God bless this child
for the love that is come.

a fiery rose

a fiery rose in a lovely garden,
a fiend to pluck it without pardon.
for we know when love is right;
do flower blossom without light?

as Satan's angels tempters know
the words they whispered soft and low
luring words I cannot tell...
go, Satan's angels back to your hell!

so they took their wings and fled
seeing how my skin burned rosy red.
these thorns and thistles would cut my hand,
to grab this rose, I could not stand!

Harriet

Harriet
wide-eyed and wonderful
fresh air to my soul
like sunflowers in a coffee can
painted by Van Gogh

call me on the cellular
tell me where you'll be
Harriet I will meet you there
buy you whiskey or a tea

spin a graceful tale
with your piano on a stage
like a ballerina on a music box
painted by Degas

show me your gallery
in the songs you sing
let me see your memories
of all the places you have been

Janice

Janice
I love you
God only knows
what you've been through
with your childlike wonder
into the lion's den
saw your reflection in the lion's eyes
but you made it through again

and I don't know what I'd do without you
every time I think of you I smile
to picture you up the river
on a far greater ship
and into the waiting secrets of the Nile

Janice
you helped me grow
showed me more beauty
than I could ever know
you were Ann Frank in Amsterdam
Audrey Hepburn in Rome
we had the last supper at McDonalds in London
gripped my hand on the turbulent flight
all the way back home

I was the one who got torn to pieces
inside that church in Florence by an unseen hand
heaven and hell were pressing in around us
to see Donatello and the Magdalene

Louvre

a black
and white
photo
of an
eclipse
of the
sun-

a light
shining through
a house
on the
prairie,
squatting
down under
a thick
heavy
darkness.

amidst the Van Gough's
Rembrandt's and Picasso's

these are
the ones
that really
moved me.

these artists' names
I didn't recognize.

and they haunt me like ghosts
until this very day...

little things

little things can give a lot of pleasure
little things can bring you so much pain
little things can change your life forever
send you up the river and bring you back again

sometimes it feels like scratching and clawing
just to gain an inch to win your case
little things can send your world spinning
and turn all sense of value on its face

I sure don't understand why people murder
or ignore the evidence to exonerate
little things can light a cold case heart on fire
and give you back loves innocence
in a twist of fate

little things like the gift of a flower
little things like a teardrop and a prayer
it's like the glue that can hold us together
a child's eyes and a fresh breath of air

there's always something

there's always something
just when you think you've won
you lose the hand of poker
you come under the gun
it's always something
just when your ship comes in
it sinks in the harbor
and you have to begin again

it's always a surprise
when the doctor brings good news
or after a million tries
you figure out the clues
and you're always asking why
you have to pay your dues
you walk out on the water
but there are holes in your shoes

you jump out of an airplane
they forgot to pack the chute
you look into someone's eyes
to see love gone destitute
whenever something's going right
there's always something going wrong
whenever the angels come around
it seems the devils always tag along

children of the light

rejoice evermore pray without ceasing
give thanks in everything you do
for this is the will of God
in Christ Jesus concerning you

for you are children of the day
not children of the night
not children of the darkness
but children of the light

and the very God of peace
sanctify you wholly
and be preserved blameless
to the coming of our Lord Jesus

put on the breastplate of faith
and salvation for a helmet
faithful is he that calls you
and he will also do it

baby shoes

baby shoes baby shoes
I'm gonna sing about baby shoes
baby shoes baby shoes
I'm gonna sing about baby shoes

first you learn to walk
then you learn how not to fall
they dip them in a bronze
and hang them on the wall

baby shoes baby shoes
I'm gonna sing about baby shoes
baby shoes baby shoes
I'm gonna sing about baby shoes

then you start to run
you grow up fast and tall
you chase the silver dollar
and you put away the doll

baby shoes baby shoes
I'm gonna sing about baby shoes
baby shoes baby shoes
I'm gonna sing about baby shoes

then you go full circle
that's when you're getting old
you learn to be child again
to walk on streets of gold

baby shoes baby shoes
I'm gonna sing about baby shoes
baby shoes baby shoes
I'm gonna sing about baby shoes

kitty cat

woe and muse, this and that,
I'll tell you a story about a cat.
he strolled into the yard one day,
and he decided that he would stay.
no one knew from where he came,
and nobody knew his name.
so we just called him kitty cat,
"here kitty, kitty cat!"

he slept inside the studio!
sprawled across the board.
he'd pounce on top of the tape machine!
just when we'd hit record.
he'd jump on top the monitor,
as if it were his throne.
with no limiter set on his domain,
and no rules to where he could not roam.

sometimes we'd see him on the lawn
chasing some imaginary prey.
or sitting on top of the bass player's car,
until he'd drive away.
or sometimes in an upstairs window,
watching like a god.
but mostly in the studio,
fiddling with a knob.

"what happened to that cymbal crash!"

or to that string part, or to that flute!"
with everyone tearing out their hair!
"Oh! It's just the kitty cat he hit the mute."
or: "How did that get in there?
I never noticed that!
that's way too much compression dear!
it must have been the cat."

the last time anyone saw him,
go gently into that good street.
he was eaten by a coyote,
and I bet he went down sweet.
so now he's up in heaven,
somewhere between flat and sharp
in the hands of an angel,
the strings on a harp!

the canyon flight

going up through the canyon
flying around the bend
to the flag on top the mountain
way at the other end
boom chukka chukka chukka
boom chukka pea
you can be the pilot
the helicopter is me

first stop is the graveyard
it's really not a grave
just bugs in a reservoir
a place we like to play
boom chukka chukka chukka
boom chukka go
I will be the engine
and you're the radio

rise above the mud path
watch out for the mud
don't be sliding back Jack
just fly up to the road
boom chukka chukka chukka
boom chukka fan
you're the navigator
and I will hold your hand

we make the water tower
on a wing and a prayer

now we're climbing higher
and we're only half way there
boom chukka chukka chukka
boom chukka fly
pull back on the stick
now we're pretty high

the trail's getting harder
that's what I call a hiker
now we're going nowhere
stuck up in the stickers
boom chukka chukka chukka
boom chukka whirl
I am the propellers
you can be the twirl

the flag is just too far
it's just too far away
we started out too late
we'll try again someday
boom chukka chukka chukka
boom chukka run
flag glowing on horizon
red white and blue we're done

we have to go back home
we have to turn around
before the mountain lion comes
and before the sun goes down
boom chukka chukka chukka
boom chukka land

flying down in the dark
don't crash and break a hand!

the Halloween parade

let's go riding in the school bus
the big bright yellow school bus
behind the ghouls marching band
in the Halloween parade

there are cowboys and Indians
ghosts and goblins
spooky dark eyed skeletons
in the Halloween parade
there are spiders in a spider's web
with eyes all glowing red
a clown's fire-truck on fire
and there goes the walking dead

they've got Shriners in little cars
tearing up the boulevard
Mickey Mouse and Hockey Duck
to help the kids not cry too hard
there are flags from Mexico
Canada and the USA
with a shrine of freemasonry
and the all-seeing evil eye

so we'll sing a song for Jesus
cause nothing here can scare us
as we remember those who've gone before
on a hallowed all saints day
so let's go riding in the school bus
in Luther's yellow school bus

like a light bulb in the darkness
in the Halloween parade

Sarah saw a snake

Sarah saw a snake!
slithering along the wall...
sssssssss sssssssss
sssssssss sssssssss

she tried to tell her daddy,
but he did not listen to her at all.
sssssssss sssssssss
sssssssss sssssssss

"noooooo daddy, it's not pretend!
the snake is really real!"
sssssssss sssssssss
sssssssss sssssssss

"I saw it over there_
it slid right past my heel!"
sssssssss sssssssss
sssssssss sssssssss

"it's right beside the house
I'm scared that it might bite..."
sssssssss sssssssss
sssssssss sssssssss

"it looked pretty in the moonlight
its colors were so bright!"
sssssssss sssssssss
sssssssss sssssssss

so we followed it with a stick...
until it slithered out of sight!
sssssssss sssssssss
sssssssss sssssssss

you should listen to your kids,
your kids just might be right.
sssssssss sssssssss
sssssssss sssssssss

I spy a big green monster alien!

I spy a big green monster alien!
it's not from the USA, or even Canadian
in a smack down with Underdog
I wonder who would win?
it's BAD! it's HORRIBLE!
it's an ODDBALL alien!

I spied it on the big screen
where everything is fake
"I'm from the planet Omeba-9,
to me...you taste like cake!"

"I came here for the food source
like Jell-O you will shake
when I turn up the heat to eat
to me...you smell like steak!"

I spy a big green monster alien
in a smack down with Batman
I wonder who would win?
stay tuned
we'll be right back!
could this really be the end?

the best day ever

we had a marshmallow roast
at a fire pit by the sea
it was the best day ever
my family friends and me
not a cloud or drop of rain
just a day to remember
a day that the Lord has made
a day to last forever

every day is the best day ever
when you have love, love for one another
when you have a father and a mother
who love you and always love each other

it started on a trampoline
we bounced in the backyard
took a walk in the canyon
up past the bug graveyard
saw a roadrunner on the road
picked wild flowers together
gave a bouquet to the angels
on the best day ever

on the best day ever
we had pizza and ice cream
watched a favorite movie
and got to ride in a limousine
we thank God for his love
and praise Him for his grace

for Jiminy Cricket solid comfort
to live in such a place

love is all there is

my father was a miner;
he worked in the underground.
we all lived in two-room shack,
by a lake outside of town.
my mother and my father
and little kids running around.
then one day tragedy struck,
and my father he went down.

love is all there is,
love is all there is.
it can bind you together,
or it can tear you apart.
but love is forever,
when love is in your heart,
love is all there is…

I've been around this whole wide world;
I've been up to the Eiffel Tower.
seen everything there is to see from there,
and I've wandered through the ruins of power.
stood out under the sky of stars,
up in the great white north.
heard the voice of God in a baby's cry,
and for all this life is worth.

love is all there is…

once I went back to the old moon town

found our house still standing there
I stared down into the black hole past
but couldn't see anything anywhere
not one memory of my father
came from the silent walls of time
just the longing to know what might have been
if daddy had come home from the mine

love is all there is...

Christ the Lord

Jesus was born in Bethlehem
Jesus was born in Bethlehem
a baby in a manger
just like the bible said

I will bow and worship him
for Jesus is the living Word
I will praise his holy name
for He is Christ the Lord

then he went down to Egypt
the child down to Egypt land
until His Father called him out
when the evil king was not at hand

then Jesus went up to Nazareth
Jesus lived in Nazareth
he shall be called a Nazarene
where He grew into a man

then He went to Jerusalem
to fulfill God's plan
Jesus wept over Jerusalem
he died and rose again

now He's up in heaven
he ascended into heaven
to the throne of the Father
and sits at Gods right hand

without names

the bridge is on fire
with the flames of desire
for all the young mothers
who would deny what's inside
and the child without reason
sinks down to the bottom
where even scavengers breed
and are carried in with the tide.

they let the whales run free
with their newborn babies
they hear the cry of the seals
and they leave them alone
but tell me where o where
are all the unwanted children
without names up in heaven
where they'll never be known.

with hearts like an iceberg
they wait by the ocean
there's a cold wind blowing
and the waves won't stand still
and the memories wash in
on the shoreline to haunt them
there's a tidal wave growing
with every child that they kill.

lady of the Mayflower

She lights up the room
when she walks in the door
with a voice like a song
she tiptoes across the floor
with the grace of a ballerina
she's a real live wire
and moves like a dancer
little lady of the Mayflower

too young to know her history
she carries like innocence
she's very special to me
in this pilgrim's progress
if John Alden could only see
America at this hour
would his dreams all come true
in this lady of the Mayflower

lady of the Mayflower
princess of the May
if he could see his little girl
I wonder what he'd say
this blossom that was planted
the first flower in the spring
when the cold winter ended
and the birds began to sing

the spelling song

C A R E
spells care
L O V E
spells love
I care for you
and I love you
you care for me
and love me too

I before E
except after C
or when sounding like A
as in neighbor and weigh
U before I
God before You
that's where you find J O Y
in Jesus Others and You

G O D
spells God
P R A Y
spells pray
I pray that God
helps me to love him and my neighbor
and keeps me in his W A Y
for that is his way.

Mary had a baby

Mary had a baby
O Mary had a baby
and his name was Jesus
O what a sight it was

Mary had a baby
O Mary had a baby
He was born in a manger
O what a sight it was

a gleam was spotted in the sky
a star shining down from on high
like a light beam from God's eye
on His newborn Son

the shepherds came to see him
the shepherds came to see him
they left their sheep behind them
O what a sight it was

then there came three wise men
then there came three wise men
with gold myrrh and frankincense
O what a sight it was

as baby Jesus got older
Mary's excitement grew
she knew he came from the Father

and longed to see what God would do

Mary had a baby
O Mary had a baby
and his name was Jesus
O what a sight it was

the rabbit hole

my daughter asked me
If I'd take her to the bookstore tonight

sure which one do you want to go to
_the one with the escalator that goes up

to the kids section or the other one

to Barns and No Bull, dad!

driving there she tells me

"it looks like there's a game at Angel Stadium
tonight"

the lights were blaring bright in the distance

"do you want me to take you to a game there this
summer?" I asked.

"no! I don't like it there. It is too loud and you
can't see what's going on,

and when I was there as a little girl I tried the
batting game and missed the ball, and some people
laughed at me. I still got a card, though."

"sweetie, " I said. " no one was laughing at you!
they just thought you were too cute! At least

you picked up the bat and swung!
hit strike or foul, you were a winner!
the greatest losers are the ones who won't even
pick up the bat to try. it's like they have a sign
hanging around their neck saying,
'DON'T TRY'!"

"well the Anaheim Angels hold a special place in
my heart, because they won the World Series the
year you were born, and I was holding you on my
shoulders when they hit the winning run!" I told
her.

"well I know why it was so special to you, and
why you were so happy then!" She chimed in.

"why is that sweetie?"

"because_that is the last time when the house was
clean!"

"Ha!"

_at the bookstore she came to me when I was
looking at a Bukowski book.

she looked at the cover and read:

"War All The Time- now why would you read
something like that!?"

"trying to keep up on the competition" I said.

(I wanted to say, "it's easier than reading a comic book, and I can keep one eye on you!" but if I said that, then she would want to read it, and I sure don't want her reading the infamous pervert wino poet!
   I read him not because I like what he says or stands for, but because he embodies both greatness and degradation . he rose to the heights and sank to the depths at the same time, then wrote about the tension in the middle that pushed him to become what he was ! he really seemed to be a mocker and a God hater!)

_then she asked me if she could sit on my knee and read to her from; 'Who Would Win In A Fight Between A Shark And A Train?'

so I did, and then off she ran to look for another book

now Bukowski would be the shark, and Duhan the train…or maybe the other way around? I can just see it;

"IN THIS CORNER WITH THE BLACK TRUNKS, COMING LIKE A FREIGHT TRAIN! THE IRON FISTED BOOZESOWSKI!

AND IN THE OTHER CORNER IN THE WHITE TRUNKS, EDDY 'THE SHARK' TWOHANDS!!

WHO CAN RHYME WITH THE LEFT AND
FREESTYLE WITH THE RIGHT!

NOW YOU GUYS KNOW THE RULES!
DUHAN KEEP IT CLEAN…BUKOWSKI
ANYTHING GOES!

When you hear the bell, come out swinging!!"

DING DING DING DONG!!

then round one was interrupted,

soon she was back studying a pop-up book of
Alice in Wonderland,

peering intently down the rabbit hole.

and there I was…

with Bukowski again,

holding the vorpal sword high in the air!

3.

a cowboy poet's stew

a homeless drifter's brew

and just a little pinchy poo

of yodel lady yodel loo

the Johnny Cash lost classic...

mama said don't ever walk that line.
you'll fall into that ring of fire
and get burned every time.
and you stand before the Devil
in the darkness of the night,
and he's only got one riddle
so you better get it right.

ah ooh,

he said, "one road leads to heaven
and one road leads to hell,
and you only get one question
so you better ask it well.
from these two men, one's a liar,
and one man tells the truth.
one road eternal fire,
one road eternal youth."

ah ooh,

well the devil started laughing
not many got it right!
but Johnny stood there thinking
and turning on the light...
then suddenly he smiled,
and told the devil what he knew.

he said, "If you were the other guy
what door would you tell me to walk through?"

ah ooh.

well the devil hung his head down,
because Johnny got it right
and the door swung right open
and he walked into the light.
because the man who was a liar
and the man who told the truth
both pointed at the same door,
and Johnny walked right through-

the opposite!

whispering

we make all our choices

never paying any mind

to all those whispering voices

farther down the line

so who did you think you'd fool

it's what you've wanted all along

there's no exception to the rule

it's either right or wrong

but I can tell that you're not listening

I can see it on your face

can you hear the words I'm whispering

are you drifting into space

now I've done just what you told me

and I've rolled away the stone

but you're the life giver

it's you and you alone

so you can take the glory

and I will take the prize

and hide it in a story

that whispers wisdom in disguise

but I can tell that you're not listening

I can see it on your face

can you hear the words He's whispering

or a you drifting into space

red dirt

you came all the way to Texas
just to be with me
but when you met all of my old buddies
you pulled the rug out from under my feet
and it took me such a long time
to believe we were really apart
when you walked out you left red dirt
on the floor of my heart

well I read all your old love letters
but they just made me cry
when you first came to see me
we were flying so high
but I never knew the reason
for the landing in the dark
when you walked out you left red dirt
on the floor of my heart

the red dirt of Texas on the floor of my heart
a stain on my memory
of what should never have been
at least I found out before it was too late
so I'll be all right if you know what I mean

when you said you'd always love me
I believed that it was true
but the way you looked at the others
what were you trying to do
I should have known long ago

what you were trying to start
when you walked out you left red dirt
on the floor of my heart

Smilin' Johnnie and his Prairie Pals

the snow was blowing hard that night,
momma put some coal in the old wood stove.
the radio say's it's going to freeze up tight,
but we got some songs to warm your soul!

we've got Smilin' Johnnie and his Prairie Pals,
Mickey and Bunny and the Polka Band.
Bobby Curtola for all the pretty young gals,
so take your partner by the hand!

we're all dancing in the living room,
my sisters, my brother, and me with a broom.
my brother says, "hey Elvis, can't get a girl?"
"I've got Annette Funichello
 coming over real soon!"

that was way back in 63,
our Saskatchewan music jubilee.
when I think about all of that history.
it seems like such a faraway dream to me...

Jesus left the 99

I was lying face down,
on the bar room floor.
and I was crying, "My God
what have I done this for?"
then I seen His hand,
reaching out to me.
there's only one place that I wanna be,
that's back in Your loving arms.

Jesus left the 99,
and went out looking for the stray.
when he found me he gave me my freedom,
took my independence away.

he said, "Son I don't want you,
living this way anymore.
if you can make it to your feet,
I know you can make it to the door.
I've seen all the places you've ever been,
and you don't know how much,
I've been hurt by your sin,
but I'll even take you just as you are."

he led me to the living waters,
and let me drink there for free.
and took me to the greenest pastures,
that this old cowboy has ever seen.
and let me ride out on His open range,
and loves to hear the praises that I sing.

ode to T.S.Eliot

the bloody sword of sunset
in the angels hand
the tale of a weeping comet
in the poet's pen.

at the still point of the turning
resolve of constellations
the vacant stage of interstellar
black holes and empty spaces.

so here I am and there are you
trying to learn the use of words
like wailing withered flowers
fall on open ears unheard.

communicate with voiceless planets
waiting in the darkness there
describe the theatre of the heavens
of time present past and future.

the curtain to implode upon us
all at once all into once
into the dotted eye of fire
where the fire and love are one.

my father

my father was a tough old miner
though I never knew him at all.

except by the stories my brother would tell me, of
the few he could recall.

for he was only five years old,
and I was only three.

when he finally left us,
slipping into eternity…

so we left our home in Sudbury,
and headed for a prairie town.

you must have been so unhappy;
we thought you'd come around.

but you grew real silent,
never did come out.

take a look in my eyes mother,
and tell me what you're thinking about.

you must have really loved him,
he must have loved you too!

tell us what he was like then,
the things you wanted to do-

my brother flies his airplanes,
me, I just play this old guitar.

my sisters are all having babies,
is that what he was hoping for?

Jesus in the balcony

I don't care if I ever make it I big on planet earth
if no one here ever knows my name
can't do that moonwalk
to grab the jewels for all I'm worth
but I love to play music just the same
so I'll sit here in the choir
like a diamond in the rough
waiting to cross over into Beulah is enough

I'll be big in New Jerusalem
and this will be a number one song
with Jesus in the balcony
and a choir of angels singing along

the first shall be last
and the last shall be first
if I don't make it here
that's the best not the worst
because I know there's a stringed instrument
waiting there for me
hand-made by the Savior
from the wood of the cross
that rings out across eternity

the Gulf of Mexico

hey you know I think about you
every single day
and I'm wondering
if you think that much of me
I've been so many places
that I can truly say
you're the best thing
I have ever seen

but I've never been down to the Gulf of Mexico
and I never did get to New Orleans
but if you want to know the truth I'm so glad I
didn't go
because you would not be here right next to me

there were times I felt as empty
as the holes in my old shoes
but walking here with you
made me forget about those blues
your eyes are like the diamonds
that sparkle on the sea
and I could walk out on the water
when you smile at me

love can break the shackles
that will bind us to our fears
and I'm so glad
our love has set us free
so let's leave them for the "trash man"

and forget about those years
He'll light the road ahead
for us to see

forever…until the cows come home

when the wind blows across the prairie
and the cold of winter is gone
it makes me think of God in his glory
and Jesus as he leads us along

we will live with him together
and we'll never be alone
in the kingdom of his green pastures
forever…until the cows come home

when the sun shines on the river
and it moves in a sparkling flight
it makes me think of God's Holy Spirit
and Jesus walking in the light

we won't need any more money
won't have to pay for our clothes
we'll drink of the living waters for free
forever…until the cows come home

go down

on a highway in Saskatchewan,

we were talking about our youth.

snow falling in the darkness

were you ever troubled by the truth?

when a car came up behind us

and turned out its lights-

was it the Devil or some killer?

so we pulled over to find out.

go down, go down in stormy weather

go down, we'll go down there together

go down, I'll go down with my brother

just like in those old days

of playing war down at the river.

so the car pulled up behind us,

we jumped out and walked their way

we wanted to see their faces

and hear what they had to say;

but they backed out on the highway

and turned their car around

and passed beside us slowly

with their window halfway down.

go down, go down in stormy weather

go down, we'll go down there together

go down, I'll go down with my brother

just like in those old days

of dancing on the frozen river.

so there's ghosts out on this highway

and our hometown is in the distance,

we're laughing at the danger

and we're smoking menthol cigarettes.

and the snow keep falling harder

to cover up all the evidence,

of all those things that we remember

like 2 soldiers of the coincidence.

go down, go down in stormy weather

go down, we'll go down there together

go down, I'll go down with my brother

just like in those old days

of baptism in the river of fire.

red dog

I've been living in the country
Lord knows I've been here before
the goats they got so hungry
went and chewed their way through the door
and the roosters won't stop crowing
it's a quarter to four
I'm living in the country again

my girl came out from the city
just the other day
my God, I think she was pretty
she had a lot to say
when she told me she was leaving
did you hear me pray
I'm living in the country again

wandering around in the open fields
I can hear a distant train
there's a red dog following at my heels
and he's stinking from the rain
I had so much I wanted to give
and I wish she felt the same
I'm living in the country again

Buddy

the last time I saw Buddy
was in the country in Washington
we sat by his campfire and I picked his old guitar
and Red Nancy was on the mandolin
he paced around like a tiger
and talked like you ain't never heard
he talked like the world was on fire
and you didn't want to miss a word

and he danced he danced all around that night
he sang us his songs and he testified
about how he was trying to hide

he talked all night about Jesus and life
he told us about the games that he was playing
and if you'd have been there to hear him
you could have reached out and touched what he
was saying
he said, Eddy, you know I could have made it
I could have traveled everywhere
and everybody thought I was crazy
ah, but I didn't really care

so I rode back to the city
with Nancy in her beat up old truck
and we couldn't help but wondering
if he knew just what he was giving up
I said Red, you know Jesus is coming
and I sure hope old Buddy will be around

cause if he ain't there to meet him
well that's one thing he ain't never gonna live
down

and he danced he danced all around that night
doing the old soft-shoe backslide

paint stray gun

PLEASE STAND BY FOR A SPECIAL
ANNOUNCEMENT:

THE LOAD STOPS HERE FOR ONE DAY
ONLY!

AIRLESS ELECTRIC PAINT SPRAYERS

TO BE SOLD TO THE PUBLIC

FOR ONE DAY ONLY!

IT WAS DISCOVERED

THAT AN ENTIRE SHIPMENT

OF AIRLESS ELECTRIC PAINT SPRAYERS

WAS MISLABELED BY THE MANUFACTURE

ALLOWING *'JOHNEDDYWAYNE'*

WHOLESALE DISTRIBUTORS

TO SELL THESE SPRAYERS

TO THE PUBLIC

FOR ONLY 20 DOLLARS EACH!

THIS SALE IS FOR ONE DAY ONLY

AND WILL BE HELD FROM

8 AM TO 8 PM

AT THE CONVENTION ROOM

OF THE HOLIDAY INN

ON HIGHWAY 10

DUE TO THE NATURE

OF THIS SALE

IT WILL BE

CASH ONLY!

Koko

I was dropping off
the rented truck
at the dealer
in Des Moines, Iowa
she was visiting her mother
who was the secretary there.
when I was leaving
she followed me out...

"Would you like to go out
for a drink with me tonight
after you get off work?" she asked me.

"Sure," I told her.

so we went to this jazz club
near the Capitol building.
we had a drink and listened to
this black lady singing
like Koko Taylor
"Beautiful absolutely beautiful!" I said.

"my mother said I shouldn't go out with you,
she said you were trying to come on to her
and that she didn't trust you."

"ha! me coming on to her, your mother?

I was just being
nice to her, and professional! I can't
believe she would even say
a thing like that!"

"that's what I told her too!"

later on she told me; "I used to
be a stripper. I ended up marrying
this dumb farmer, and it didn't work out
so I left him..."

and then she said

"I grew up in Texas-
we lived next door to this airline pilot
when I was 14 he raped me and I got pregnant!
I had an abortion.
since then I've had 7 abortions..."

after another drink…

"I bet you have only one thing on your mind,"
she said to me. "You just want to have sex with
me!"

"well not really!"

"well then why did you agree
to come out with me then?"

"well, because you asked me,
and you seemed lonely.
I feel sorry for you."

"I wish you wouldn't have said that!
I really wish you wouldn't have said that." She
said.

(I wished I hadn't said it either...)
then she picked up her blue coat
and walked out.

while Koko's sound alike belted out:

"love me baby love me..."

so very very sad.

heroes

all the old war heroes
come together again
they talk about the sorrow
they talk about the pain.
all the old war heroes
come together once more
they talk about the legends
and the tales of the war...

they came one day from battle,
all weary and torn apart.
with a burning desire for freedom,
in the darkness of their hearts.

you can find them in the lonely rooms,
remembering the wars.
where no one ever goes.
locked behind closed doors.
or sitting like an empty glass,
in the cheap hotel bars,
cigarette burns on red vinyl stools,
with bullet holes and scars.

all the old war heroes
came together again,
they've felt all the sorrows
they've felt all the pain.
all the old war heroes
when will they close the door?

for the only sons they had
have gone off to the war.

romance novel

the pages of your favorite romance novel
turned yellow from the sun
so I left it there on my rear window
when I abandoned my old car
those pages were just too painful
I couldn't read Jane Eyre

_love is like that sometimes
when your heart is hard and hateful
and you don't know who you are

I got a letter from somewhere in Italy
saying you hated it where you were
sometimes I wish I had sent you the money
to help you get away from there
but I remembered what you said
the last time that you saw me
you didn't want me to care

_love is like that sometime
when your heart is hard and hateful
and you don't know where you are

you resisted all the way
and it really tore me apart
but there was a price I couldn't pay
my obsession for your unhappy heart

that was the last time that I saw you

I never thought I'd hear from you again
but there's twist in every story
a twist for each and every turn
I let go when it was finally over
then you tried to hold on in the end

_love is like that sometimes
when your heart is hard and hateful
and you don't know why you are

time slips away

15 years old

and I was on the road

it was wintertime in Canada

the snow was blowing cold

but I couldn't shake

that feeling in my soul

it seemed every place I left behind

was the same as where I'd go

I met Jesus in Vancouver

when I was all alone

at his house by the river

from a seawall for a home

and that's where he spoke to me

and told me he was real

at the time I didn't have much

and I was looking for a meal

He said look at the sky

and know that I Am He

if you open your eyes

it's so easy to see

that the mountains in the distance

we created by me

and my thoughts of you

have been more than the sands of the sea

well it sure feels good

to be back here again

I never thought I'd be lost for words

but I don't know what to say

except Thank You

for making it ok

and time slips away

like satin through your fingers

but the memory stays

like a sweet dream that lingers

and never goes away

Flannery's place

it would be great
to cross that wave,
and to visit the Andalusian
to see the colors
at Flannery¹s Place,
in her peacock garden…

to hear the story that she tells,
that can¹t be told by anyone else,
to hear the black bird clap its wings.
to the rhythm of the times.
drive home the point that Greenleaf brings,
when a good man is hard to find.

I have felt all her words,
like the burning in the cotton.
and I yearn for just one more,
and search for one lost or forgotten.
of the heroine in the slave.
of her redemption in the grave.

the story that was never written.

ghosts on the prairie

we drove the cattle north,
from the Mexican border.
the wind was hot and thirsty,
it drank up all the water.

the winter came too early,
we got caught out in the storm!
stranded in the canyon,
just trying to keep warm.

Billy caught sick;
died on Christmas Day.
so we just crossed some sticks,
for a headstone on his grave.

it left a deep impression,
burning in our minds,
saying, "Jesus won't you help us
through these times?"

through these times
through these times
Jesus won't you help us through these times

if we ever make it back,
make it back alive!
I'm never riding drag,

on another cattle drive.

but if we never make it back,
and we cross that Great Divide
we'll be the ghosts that haunt the prairie
until we reach the other side

land of the living skies

I went for a walk in the country
where there are no people or cars
down the ancient path by the river
under the bright dome of stars

hey hey hey
it's a sign of our Saviors grace

when the wind blows over the prairie
it feels like a song sometimes
with only the thoughts that you carry
into the land of the living skies

hey hey hey
it's a song of our Saviors grace

were only here for a short time
the centuries are gone and plowed under
if I come back here in a billion more years
I know I will always remember

hey hey hey
it's the time of our Saviors grace

I love to travel

I love to travel
the world over
see old great cultures
everywhere
the sky seems different
over every country
it's like a fingerprint
way up there.

but most of all
I love to travel with you
to see that look in your eyes
when you see something old
like something new!

the Coliseum
the Eiffel Tower
Lenin's tomb
in Red Square
the ancient churches
the new spring flowers
the busy markets
in the open air…

something old like something new
something unique and something true
to see that look on your face
I love to travel with you!

I scare myself

I scare myself
every time I stare into the mirror on the wall
with those fly buggy eyes
and that twisted kind of Frankenstein smile
I scare myself

I scare myself
creeping through the jungle in my mind
not knowing what I'm looking for
never sure about what I'm going to find
I scare myself

hey look out someone's coming!
duck into the trees don't let them know
but there ain't no use in running
cause there isn't any place that you can go

I scare myself
every time I take a walk inside
you'd think I was Dr. Jekyll
I got news for you I'm Mr. Hyde
I scare myself

I scare myself
every time I look inside my head
I scare myself
I've been to places angels fear to tread
I scare myself
you find me hiding underneath the bed

I scare myself
so please forget everything that I just said!

top heavy

that top heavy
golden image
serpents head
will spin that body right around
those ten toes
will look like crowns
when that serpent
hits the ground
and hanging naked upside down
as it begins to sway
its face covered by a gown
behold the beast of iron and clay_
the clay of soft tyranny
mixed with the iron of false morality.

love is a door

love is a door on Noah's Ark
love is a window on the third story
when the flood comes love will keep us warm
and carry you away with me.

and there shall be a bow in the clouds
of colors to remember
Stretching across that big wide sky
like a heart of love forever…

love is a bond between a man and a woman
love is the command of the Lord to them
love is when the rains began
and the hand of the Lord shut them in.

love is for the promise that was made
for as long as the earth remains
love is for the cold in the winter
day and night summer and the spring

open road song

I traveled the roads in North California
long and winding through the tall redwood trees
I made my way from Toronto to Vancouver
and read all the road signs that stand in between

and sometimes it was such a hard road to travel
sometimes I thought I would lose more than gain
then Jesus came and put me
on the straight and narrow
and it's better than that highway
to fortune and fame

made my way in Greyhound buses
walked the dark highways that seemed so far
lit out across the wheat fields and orchards
where a farmhouse light shines like a star

I made my way down that long open road
going God's way and singing His songs
made my way beyond that long dusty highway
toward God's holy city my eternal home

4.

Waiting for the big resolve...

remember

before the silver chord is broken
and the golden bough is crushed
the pitcher by the well is shattered
and everything returns to dust

remember your Creator
before the evil days are come
when the stars are all darkened
and there is no light in them

and the daughters will sing softly
and the grasshopper drags himself along
while the mourners go about the streets
and a man to his eternal home

a new day

You're like the morning breeze
rustling through the trees
as I walk this country road and think of you
I would have counted all the stars last night
but the sun came through and hid their light
so I guess I must have missed one or two

it's a new day with you
I'm not feeling blue
like the sky up above
so I'll whistle you a tune
like a whippoorwill in June
cause I'm in love with you

You're like the running stream
it's where I sit and dream
about the day I'll get to see your smiling face
with eyes shining like the sun
the new morning just begun
and the footprints swept away without a trace

it's a new day with you
I'm not feeling blue
like the sky up above
so I'll whistle you a tune
like the crazy loon
cause I'm in love with you

there's a symphony of crickets

and frogs down by the pond
there's a blue jay in the thickets
with a love song from beyond

I see Jesus

I see Jesus
in the promise of Abraham
I see Jesus
in the burning tree
I see Jesus
in the furnace with the children
I see Jesus when he died for me

He brings back
love from the grave
He brings back
life and redemption
and great power to save

I see Jesus
in baby Moses on the river
I see Jesus
crossing the Red Sea
I see Jesus
walking on the water
I see Jesus when he set me free

Jesus in the lion's den
Jesus in Noah's ark
Jesus in Jonah's whale
Jesus in my heart

the one hope for fallen sinners is the crucified Lord

to you O victor pierced by nails
on the cross calls out to sinners
saying come freely receive forgiveness
to you I lift unrelenting prayers

O my savior turn away your eyes
from all my lawlessness
by your sufferings heal my sores
that I may glorify your kindness

O all-good one
whose kindness is greater
than the deceit of the world

strengthen my miserable soul with hope
in Thy kindness for it is weak
it holds on only by your mercy
and it hopes to find comfort in Thee

I hope in your mercies

bad habits entangle me like snares
I sink to the very depths of evil
I rejoice at being bound
so daily the enemy gives me new shackles

I appear to be robed in the beautiful clothes
but my soul is entangled in shameful thoughts
to all who might see I appear composed
but inside I am filled with bitter loss

I hope in your mercies I fall at your feet
lead my soul out of iniquity
may a ray of light shine in my mind
Lord Jesus Christ have mercy on me

how pitiful I am in my daily repentance
for it has no firm foundation.
every day I lay a stone on the building
and with my own hand cause its destruction

no one can heal my disease

No one can heal my disease
except for him who knows the heart
how many times have I set boundaries
and then my will tore the walls apart
again I knock at the door
that it may open up for me
I do not cease to ask for grace
I know no shame in seeking mercy

rouse your strength and come
like a beam of lightening
disperse the power of my enemy
O Lord that you might save me

wrench me from the mire
that I may not be stained forever
deliver me from the lion's jaws
Who's seeking who he may devour
as soon as he sees your face
he is taken back with fear
and now my master save me
for to you I flee in prayer

hands of chaos

hooray, hooray for the side that won,
hooray, hooray for nobody at all!

soldiers marching like a metronome,
tanks crawling through city streets with hypnotic
drone.

and the land is torn apart with the hands of chaos,
and becomes the prey for the vulture corporations.

and a nuclear madness sweeps the nations,
if you're lucky enough to see the dust clear you'll
end up with nothing.

but who is wrong and who is right?
they will bury justice and decide it by might...

so hooray, hooray for the Silent One,
hooray, hooray for when the Lord takes all!

Mary

I'm talking to my sister,
she's crawling up a hill.
I can't carry that cross for you,
I know it's such a bitter pill.
but I've stolen off the altar,
and I drank the holy wine.
and I strangled my last sacrament,
when I was only nine.
and I say, "Mary, is that really you?"

I walking by the river,
and I'm thinking about your will.
and I can hear this voice beside me;
I can even hear it still.
it said, "I have this will for you."
the words they even rhymed,
it said, "Someday you will know it too,
your just too young and blind!"
and I say, "Mary, is that really you?"

and I miss those times,
we were together alone.
you were the sound of the wind,
and I was the hollow bone.
I was Judas picking pockets,
down in the catacombs.
you were the killer in high places,
of principalities and thrones.
is that really you?

I met Jesus in the 60's,
I fell in love with Joan of Arc,
but she left with someone younger,
and the 70's were all dark.
in the 80's I felt paralyzed,
I still carry all the scars.
but I found out who is the Antichrist,
it was written in the stars.
and I say, "Mary, is that really you?"

dark day

there's a dark day a dark day
coming this here way
there's an ill wind blowing through the land
hear the black dog howling in the distance
for him who has ears to understand

there's a dark day a dark day
coming this here way
you can feel it everywhere
I thank Jesus that I'm not going to stay
I'm going to fly away on a wing and a prayer

so you can eat drink and be merry
and you can kiss away your time
but just remember the water
that he turned into wine
and remember the fish
and the 5 loaves of bread
or how he died on the cross
and he rose up from the dead

and remember it all
and remember it well
don't say I didn't warn you
when you're down the road to hell!

postcard

Like a postcard from long ago,
an asteroid hit this ground;
killed off all the dinosaurs,
and it became a mining town.

a mining town called Sudbury,
way up in North Ontario.
the tallest smokestack in the world,
and hot oak fires from down below.

the devil works the crusher
to break the metal from the rock.
like Baudelaire in the fire
to the rhythm of the clock.

it seems we have all forgotten,
that day in that first earth age,
when all the sons of God shouted for joy,
and the cornerstone was laid.

it's like that little yellow canary,
that broke loose from the cage of the children.
and flew all over the mining camp lake,
looking for something from someone.

April

it was so nice to meet you!
on that ferry across the Georgian Bay.
sometimes I believe in love at first sight,
and wished we didn't live so far away…

we were Pinky and the Blue Boy,
set free from the gallery wall.
angels all around in quiet repose,
as we went walking down the hall.

now you have your life, and I have mine.
you're in the water
while I'm in the air.
I'll never forget those beautiful eyes!
like wildflowers,
yet so full of care.

poetry in 7 languages,
that's what gave you away,
paradise lost in epigrams and images,
and I wish we had had the whole day!

April and me
could it be?
is it the song
we've waited for_
so long,

new travelers

travelers move
across the shining sky
full of wonder
climbing high
shining like the stars
against the dark
sea of glass
Noah's ark
rain falling
waters rising high
mixed with fire
pouring from the sky.

new travelers
speed of light
wings in motion
burning bright.
new travelers
flash of light.
world fades out
like a storm tossed night.

time framed space
surrounds the shining sky
worlds in view
through silent eyes
new horizons open
lost in flight
out of time

fade from sight.
strain to see bright visions
in their eyes
travelers move
beyond the wall outside.

signet ring

Squeeze a stone,
make it bleed.

metal blood,
power and greed.

tower of steel,
signet ring.

plutonium bomb,
devils wing.

cut a tree,
and make it burn.

ah, the fire!
keep us warm.

to fashion bibles,
or child porn?
carve a statue-
of Christ torn.

I feel it is heaven

I feel it is heaven to please you
to be what you would have me to be
pure as Christ is pure
holy as you are holy

be pleased to live and move in me
breathing in my prayers
inhabiting my praises
and speaking in my words

I feel it is heaven to embrace you
to know the love you have planted in me
before I loved you
you first loved me

Your bountiful goodness has helped me believe
awoke my faith to a glowing flame
moving in my actions
and causing me to grow in grace

Daniel prayed...

Daniel prayed in the lion's den
Jonah prayed in the belly of the whale
Elijah prayed and the fire came down
Joshua prayed and the sun stood still

God be merciful to me a sinner
not my will but Thine be done
speak for your servant is listening
here I am send me

Enoch prayed and he was no more
Noah prayed and God shut the door
Gideon prayed and he saw the sign
Samson prayed though his eyes were blind

and God restored Job
when he prayed for his friends
and gave him twice as much
as he had in the end

for Vic

we played pool at Hollywood Sound
then she took me to her place
somewhere up in Laurel Canyon,
a rare jewel of mercy and grace!
I asked her if she'd sing for me;
she smiled and said, "o.k."
so I sat down at her feet
as she began to play.

"It's something I've been working on,
it really isn't done."
then with the voice of an angel,
she sang, "Harry went to heaven."
well Harry went to heaven,
and for a moment so did I!
Harry went to heaven,
and I know why...

then we listened to her answering machine,
to some guy in love with ducks!
he was calling from the rain in Spain,
she said, "Did he say ducks or did he say trucks?"
then she picked his shoe up off the floor,
smiled and said, "Oh that guy John!
he's on the road in a band called Giant Sand,
he's such a card when he is gone!"

as we drove back down to Hollywood,
the rain was coming down!

she said, "everybody I know hates it here,
but you know I love this town!"
then I saw her one time after that,
when she invited me to her show.
at the time I was so twisted up inside,
that I went, but I didn't let her know...
and sat there in the darkness,
while she sang, "Harry went to heaven!"

Wyoming

flying,
down the highway
in the middle of nowhere. I am asleep in the
passenger seat

1:00 am:

I am awakened!
by John the Mortician! (who liked the smell of
skunk…)

screaming! At the top of his lungs
WERE GONNA DIE! WERE GONNA DIE!

WHAT? Did we hit black ice?

get caught in a tail wind?

spinning, spinning
spinning out of control!
over a 150 foot cliff!

"JESUS!"
was all that I could pray.

and so we glided down
as if in slow-motion
soft as a feather
and landed on a pillow of snow,

on all four tires.

we got out, intact.

then climbed up the cliff
and in the cold
starlit darkness
saw the silhouette
of an eighteen wheeler,
lying on its side across the highway
looking like a downed buffalo
on the Wyoming prairie...

I can't make the connection

It sure feels strange,
running into you this way.
it was such a long time ago,
I don't know what to say.
except how are you doing?
and where have you been?
doesn't 1969 seem so far away?

remember the time,
we held each other's hand?
and walked all around the seawall,
and you talked about Japan.
it was good to be there,
I wanted to stay.
then we drifted away from each other,
like the ships on the bay...

or that Sunday in the rain,
do you remember when?
we sat in your car and I sang for you,
and it was 7 a.m.
like the seasons we've changed,
and have come around again.
burning like the sun's bright flame,
and stronger for our Savior's name...

and I can't make the connection,
between then and now.
but I guess it doesn't matter anyhow.

Rosey

Rosey,
yer the only gal fer me!
Rosey,
you're the only one I see.
when I close my eyes.

I call you on the telephone,
you tell me that you gotta go.
all your pots are boiling over,
and the dinners on the stove.

Rosey...

just tell your mother that I love her,
I'll lay flowers on your father's grave.
I wish that I could reach you,
but I know only Jesus saves.

did I ever tell you you're my heroine,
even though you never let me in.
when the winter of your life is over,
maybe I'll see you in the spring...

leave me here

leave me here

to think a little

of things to come

upon the world

to contemplate

the universe

to see the stars

of heaven swirl

Arcturus, Orion,

Pleiades

the chambers

of the South

wonders without

number

and things

past finding out.

the Count

when the Count drops his pants
he never feels his shame
he rules the world with an iron hand
and no one even knows his name

I guess God has people
God has people
God has some very unfortunate people
for the negative side of His plan

he is the Flying Dutchman
he is the world's most evil man
the black pope of the underground
he carries out the Devils plan

they say he killed the Kennedy's
they say he ordered 911
and every dark deed in between
was even done by him

some even say he's alien
a serpent seed reptilian
he's never had a woman's love
just little boys and other men

a day of clouds

blow a trumpet, sound an alarm!
for the day of the Lord is near
a day of darkness, a day of clouds
never has there been any like it before.

return to the Lord with all your heart
He is gracious and full of compassion
who knows if he will not turn and relent
and leave a blessing behind him.

His army is mighty they obey his voice
they run on a city run on a wall
the sky trembles the earth shakes
the sun is darkened the stars will fall.

the waters saw you
psalm 77

in the day of my trouble
I was too troubled to speak
I cried out to you with my voice
and you gave ear to me

the waters saw you
the waters saw you
they were in anguish
the deeps also trembled
the clouds poured down water
with the sound of thunder

your lightening lit up the world
your path led through the sea
the earth trembled and shook
though your footprints were not seen

I will remember my song in the night.
I will remember your wonders of old
you led your people by your right hand
by your strength you were made known

the last trumpet

now to the coming of our Lord Jesus Christ
and our gathering together unto to him
that you might not be soon shaken
that the day of Christ is at hand

at the last trumpet
we shall all be changed
at the last trumpet
we shall all be raised
at the last trumpet
we shall never die
at the last trumpet
in the twinkling of an eye

He shall be revealed from heaven
with his angels in flaming fire
to consume with the spirit of his mouth
and destroy with the brightness of his coming

we shall not all sleep
we shall see a mystery
O death where is your sting
O grave where is your victory

the prayer of Manasseh

almighty Lord God of our fathers
heaven and earth you have made
you fettered the sea and shut up the deep
and sealed it with your glorious name

I have sinned Lord I have sinned
I have no relief and provoked you to anger
forgive me O Lord forgive me
and do not be angry with me forever

I am unworthy to look up to heaven
I am weighed down under my sins
now therefore I bend the knee of my heart
and beg for mercy in all my transgressions

I will praise you as long as I live
you are the God of those who repent
all the host of heaven sing praises
for yours is the glory forever Amen

psalm 151

my hand made an instrument
my fingers tuned the harp strings
and who will declare it to my Lord?
the Lord himself is listening.

He himself sent his messenger
He took me from my father's sheep
the youngest and the smallest child
And anointed me with his anointing oil.

I went out to meet the enemy
and he called curses down on me
but I pulled out his own sword
and with it I removed his head.

creation song

He wraps himself in light
as with a garment,
He spreads out the heavens
and walks on the wings of the wind.

He sends forth the springs
from the valleys
they flow between mountains.
the birds of the air dwell
by the waters,
lifting their voices in song-

singing glory, glory!
glory to the Lamb!
all praises and honor forever.

He made the moon for its seasons,
the sun knows its setting.
He looks at the Earth and it trembles,
He touches the mountains
and they smoke.

I will sing to the Lord all my life,
I will sing praises to my God-
as long as I live,
praises to the Lord, oh my soul.

for whomsoever will

Lucifer drew a third
of the angel's
and cast them
down to the earth
among them were such souls
as Adam and Eve,
Hitler, and Hemmingway,
and Mrs. Butterworth.

look into the mirror
all the souls were here
like Jonah in the whale
and there's misery if you fail

in fact everyone who came
poured into flesh bodies
born here in innocence
through woman and man
came with a death sentence
for their own rebellion
with a chance of redemption
as part of God's plan.

and God Himself came
in the person of Christ
and took our death sentence
on his own head
and led captivity captive

back up to the heavens
when he died on the cross
and rose from the dead.

rich man's struggle

I went to a wedding in a backyard in Bel Air
to do sound for a singer
with The Homeless Drifters PA
Harry Belafonte's daughter
was getting married
the sun was shining It was a beautiful day!

from the Hollywood skyline
came many bright stars
Kirk Douglas, Sidney Poitier,
and the dog-faced Commish
with a hit show ego as big and fat as his cigar
holding two blonde silver-dressed escorts
that sparkled like fish.

there was baby squid salad
to put on your plate,
and I talked to "Mr. Gina"
about the rich man, poor man struggle
he seemed to think that the rich had it hard
when they had to wait
or when you get beat out of a part,
that was his idea of trouble…

I said "the poor man struggles
all his life for a chance
and has nothing to fall back on
if he loses the spin…
at least the rich man still has

his comfort and money,
and will get the next one
when it comes around again…and again."

"I guess you have a point there." he conceded,
as he puffed on his cigar.

just then a big commotion
came from the front yard
everyone got up and went out to see
it stopped the wedding cold
and left the bride crying hard
saying, "WHAT'S GOING ON!
WHAT'S HAPPENING, DADDY?"

I followed Harry and the crowd
out to the front yard
to find the valet fighting
with a rent a cop in the street
apparently, they never acquired the permits
to park all the cars
so the rent a cop was ticketing everyone
as part of her beat.

the valet grabbed the ticket book
from out of her hand
and threw it away somewhere into the bushes
needless to say that was a terrible plan
as it heated up into a screaming battle
between the two witches!

the cops were called
and the tow trucks were summoned,
not even Harry Belafonte
could wave his name
like a magic wand!

everyone was told they had to park
down at the bottom
of the hill in the
Elementary schoolyard…
so the parade of international
movie stars in black tuxedos
swarmed downward
like agitated flies
until they disappeared
and were gone.

two chord voodoo

hey hey Johnny what do you say
what do you got going on today
can you come on out to play
you can drive the blues away

say hey Johnny what do you hear
slide guitar on a bottle of beer
angels singing in your ear
you can make it through another year

soar above the milky way
slide down to the muddy delta bay
you know how to make it pay
play "Jesus saved me from the miry clay"

you've heard of John the Revelator
John the Baptist in the river
Johnny Walker undertaker
that two chord voodoo of John Lee Hooker

hey hey Johnny what do you say
what do you got going on today
can you come on out to play
you can drive the blues away

drifting underneath the stars

a poet sees the poetry.
a carpenter the frame,
an astronomer the astronomy.
Plato sees shadows in the cave…
I lay here in the darkness,
and wonder at this feeling.
to see these constellations
plastered on the ceiling.

drifting underneath the stars
on a sea of dreams.
drifting underneath the stars
nothing is the way it seems.

I dreamed I was inside a painting,
framed in cage of bone.
on the open waters raging,
casting shadows from the moon.
wondering if the dead who knew us,
see a lifeboat or a coffin.
and stretching out full length to view us,
sail away to rags or fortune...

and I saw them slide like quicksilver
streaming down the walls.
on a molten sea towards forever
whom the Son of Man recalls.

waiting for the big resolve

we were at a friend's house

on the 4th of July for a pool party
and a fireworks display.

my daughter was sitting
at a round table
with a bunch of her friends.

the parents were sitting at another.

I was sitting on the back steps by myself.

my daughter turned around to me
with a big smile on her face and said,
so everyone could hear_

"hey dad, why are all men like flies?".

everybody stopped talking
and turned to look at me,
waiting to see
how I would respond.

the parents were probably thinking_
'now, why would your daughter think of,
and ask something like that?'
and the kids were probably thinking_

'is it because they are stinky and annoying?'

So, I just recited
the next line of the poem:

"they are caught in the web of the world's lies."

everyone broke out into laughter...

then as quick as they landed,
they turned and were gone.

words buzzing and circling
like flies around meat

and I just sat there

quietly waiting

waiting for the sky to explode!

waiting for the big resolve,

waiting for...

the end.

At that time Jesus answered and said, I thank thee, O Father, Lord of heaven and earth, because thou hast hid these things from the wise and prudent, and hast revealed them unto babes. Matt.11:25.

Photo by Jan Duhan

"The One Hope for Fallen Sinners", "I Hope In Your Mercies",
"No Can Heal My Disease", adapted from Ephrem the Syrian, a
4th century hymn writer.

"Besieged by Bukowski" adapted from 'Besieged' by Charles Bukowski

"Baby Shoes, "Sarah Saw A Snake", and "Mary Had A Baby"
Co-written with Sarah Elizabeth Duhan.

Long Lake Publishing
longlakemusic@yahoo.com

www.ingramcontent.com/pod-product-compliance
Lightning Source LLC
Chambersburg PA
CBHW031545040426

42452CB00006B/198